Full STEAM Ahead!

Technology Time

Think Like a Computer Scientist

Cynthia O'Brien

CRABTREE
PUBLISHING COMPANY
WWW.CRABTREEBOOKS.COM

Title-Specific Learning Objectives:

Readers will:

- Define what a computer scientist is and explain the job they do.
- Describe the different ways computer scientists think, and identify how they can think in similar ways.
- Make connections between ways that a computer scientist thinks and everyday tasks or examples.

High-frequency words (grade one)	Academic vocabulary
are, is, it, like, make, the, they, to, us, what, you	computer scientist, instructions, patterns, technology

Before, During, and After Reading Prompts:

Activate Prior Knowledge and Make Predictions:
Have children look at the cover image and the image on the title page. Spark interest in the topic by asking children what they see in the pictures. Ask them if they have ever arranged a puzzle, made pieces fit together, or created a pattern. Then, help activate prior knowledge by asking them:

- What do you think patterns, pieces, or puzzles have to do with technology?

During Reading:
After reading pages 16 and 17, ask children to consider how the examples of problem solving relate to how computer scientists think. Encourage them to make connections between earlier concepts in the book and the everyday examples given here. Prompt them with questions such as:

- How does building with blocks/growing plants show ways to think like a computer scientist?
- In what other ways do you think like a computer scientist?

After Reading:
Have children choose a way that they can show that they think like a computer scientist. They could create a pattern, write instructions for a task, break up a problem into parts, etc. Have a gallery walk in which children share their ideas.

Author: Cynthia O'Brien

Series Development: Reagan Miller

Editor: Janine Deschenes

Proofreader: Melissa Boyce

STEAM Notes for Educators: Janine Deschenes

Guided Reading Leveling: Publishing Solutions Group

Cover, Interior Design, and Prepress: Samara Parent

Photo research: Samara Parent

Production coordinator: Katherine Berti

Photographs:
iStock: FatCamera: p10, 11, 16; Highwaystarz-Photography: p18
Shutterstock: Pavel L Photo and Video: p21
All other photographs by Shutterstock

Library and Archives Canada Cataloguing in Publication

Title: Think like a computer scientist / Cynthia O'Brien.
Names: O'Brien, Cynthia (Cynthia J.), author.
Description: Series statement: Full STEAM ahead! | Includes index.
Identifiers: Canadiana (print) 20190133813 |
Canadiana (ebook) 20190133856 |
ISBN 9780778764533 (softcover) |
ISBN 9780778764076 (hardcover) |
ISBN 9781427123596 (HTML)
Subjects: LCSH: Computer science—Juvenile literature. |
LCSH: Computer scientists—Juvenile literature. |
LCSH: Problem solving—Juvenile literature. |
LCSH: Creative thinking—Juvenile literature.
Classification: LCC QA76.23 .O27 2019 | DDC j004—dc23

Library of Congress Cataloging-in-Publication Data

Names: O'Brien, Cynthia (Cynthia J.), author.
Title: Think like a computer scientist / Cynthia O'Brien.
Description: New York : Crabtree Publishing Company, 2019. |
Series: Full STEAM ahead! | Includes index.
Identifiers: LCCN 2019023733 (print) | LCCN 2019023734 (ebook) |
ISBN 9780778764076 (hardcover) |
ISBN 9780778764533 (paperback) |
ISBN 9781427123596 (ebook)
Subjects: LCSH: Computer science--Vocational guidance--Juvenile literature.
Classification: LCC QA76.25 .O26 2019 (print) | LCC QA76.25 (ebook) | DDC 004.023--dc23
LC record available at https://lccn.loc.gov/2019023733
LC ebook record available at https://lccn.loc.gov/2019023734

Printed in Canada/052022/CPC20220521

Table of Contents

Crabtree Publishing Company
www.crabtreebooks.com 1-800-387-7650

In Canada: We acknowledge the financial support of the Government of Canada through the Book Publishing Industry Development Program (BPIDP) for our publishing activities.

Published in Canada
Crabtree Publishing
616 Welland Ave.
St. Catharines, Ontario
L2M 5V6

Published in the United States
Crabtree Publishing
PMB 59051
350 Fifth Avenue, 59th Floor
New York, New York 10118

Published in the United Kingdom
Crabtree Publishing
Maritime House
Basin Road North, Hove
BN41 1WR

Published in Australia
Crabtree Publishing
Unit 3 – 5 Currumbin Court
Capalaba
QLD 4157

Computer Scientists

Computer scientists are people who use **technology** to solve problems.

This game does not work the way it should. Computer scientists can fix it. First, they find the problem. An **instruction** is wrong! Instructions tell the computer what to do.

The computer scientists think about how the game should work. They give the computer a new instruction. Now, people can have fun playing the game!

A Way to Think

Computer scientists find ways to make technology work better. They think of easier or safer ways to do jobs. They **invent** ways to make life fun! Did you know that you can think like a computer scientist too?

You think like a computer scientist when you sort things to make them easier to find.

Thinking like a computer scientist helps us solve problems and finish jobs.

You think like a computer scientist when you plan a shopping list. The shopping list helps you gather the food quickly. It helps you make sure you do not forget anything!

Solving Problems

Computer scientists break up problems into small parts. They find the part that causes the problem. Imagine your bike is broken. Let's break the problem into small parts.

Look at each part of the bike. Which part is broken?

The tires need more air!

After you fix each tire, your bike is ready to ride!

Look for Patterns

Computer scientists look for **patterns**. Patterns can show which small parts will fix a problem. Patterns can show which **steps** work well to do a job. We follow patterns too! One example is when we play sports.

First, one player passes the ball to another player. Then, the player kicks the ball. If the ball goes in the net, they score!

What happens if a teammate does not pass the ball? The pattern does not work. We **repeat** the patterns that help us win!

What is Important?

Computer scientists **focus** on the most important parts of the problem. What do we need to know to fix the problem? Which parts can we leave out?

Imagine you need to pack your backpack for the school day. What do you need to bring to school?

It is important to pack your lunch.
It is important to pack your homework.

Is it important to pack these toys to play with at recess?

Step by Step

Computer scientists make instructions for computers. They write clear steps to do a job or fix a problem. We make and follow instructions too!

A **recipe** is a set of instructions. We follow each step to make tasty food.

Games have steps to follow. These steps make the game fun to play. Have you ever helped a friend learn a game? How did you explain the instructions?

Putting it Together

When you think like a computer scientist, you can get jobs done!

You can build things with the parts you need and remove the parts you do not need.

You can make things grow by following steps! First, we put a plant in soil in a sunny place. Then, we add water. After we do these steps, the plant will grow. We can repeat the pattern for each plant.

Your Turn

Are you thinking like a computer scientist? Let's find out!

Make a set of dance steps for your friends. What parts does your dance have? Put them in order. Does your dance have a pattern that repeats?

Write down instructions that will teach your friends the dance. Try following the instructions by yourself first. Do you need to fix any problems?

Making it Work

Everyone works together to try the dance. But something is not working! Look at the dance steps one by one. Which step is causing the problem?

Only one person can do this move! How do you solve the problem?

Take out the move that you do not need. Now, the dance works!

Words to Know

focus [FOH-k*uhs*] verb To concentrate or center in on something

instruction [in-STRUHK-sh*uh*n] noun A set of steps that tells us how to do something

invent [in-VENT] verb To create something new

patterns [PAT-turns] noun Something that happens over and over again

recipe [RE-sip-ee] noun A plan for making food

repeat [ree-PEET] verb To say, do, or make something again

steps [steps] noun Actions that happen after one another, often to meet a goal or do a job

technology [tek-NOL-uh-jee] noun The tools that help us do work

A noun is a person, place, or thing.

A verb is an action word that tells you what someone or something does.

An adjective is a word that tells you what something is like.

Index

About the Author

Cynthia O'Brien has written many books for young readers. It is fun to help make a technology like a book! Books can be full of stories. They also teach you about the world around you, including other technologies.

To explore and learn more, enter the code at the Crabtree Plus website below.

www.crabtreeplus.com/fullsteamahead

Your code is:
fsa20

STEAM Notes for Educators

Full STEAM Ahead is a literacy series that helps readers build vocabulary, fluency, and comprehension while learning about big ideas in STEAM subjects. *Think Like a Computer Scientist* helps readers make connections between main ideas and examples in the text. The STEAM activity below helps readers extend the ideas in the book to build their skills in technology and the arts.

Make Instructions like a Computer Scientist

Children will be able to:

- Understand how computer scientists create clear and focused instructions to complete tasks.
- Write and illustrate step-by-step instructions that will help a peer complete an activity.

Materials

- "How to ______" Sheet
- "How to ______" Completed Example
- Whiteboard with markers

Guiding Prompts

After reading *Think Like a Computer Scientist*, ask children:

- Who are computer scientists? What do they do? Review pages four to seven.
- What are some ways computer scientists think, in order to do jobs and solve problems? Prompt children to identify the following: break down a problem, focus on the most important parts, find and follow patterns, and make step-by-step instructions.

Activity Prompts

Brainstorm ways that children follow instructions in their daily lives. Write down the ideas on the whiteboard. Then, ask children if they have ever written instructions for someone else. Talk about what makes good instructions. Refer to the concepts in the book: instructions are clear, they only include the most important parts, and they often include patterns that are easy to repeat.

Hand each child a "How to _____" Sheet and explain that they will write step-by-step instructions that will help someone take part in one of their favorite activities. Give some examples such as hitting a baseball, playing hide-and-seek, or painting a picture. Explain that each step should be accompanied by a drawing that will show their peers exactly how to complete the step. Have children complete the sheets and present the instructions to their peers.

Extensions

- Have children bring in the necessary materials and let them try out the instructions. A parent note may be required to gather materials from home. Have children talk about which parts of the instructions worked well, and which parts could be improved. Allow children to make improvements.

To view and download the worksheets, visit **www.crabtreebooks.com/resources/printables** or **www.crabtreeplus.com/fullsteamahead** and enter the code **fsa20**.